N. E. Foard

The Strangers' Guide in Baltimore and its Environs

N. E. Foard

The Strangers' Guide in Baltimore and its Environs

ISBN/EAN: 9783337180959

Printed in Europe, USA, Canada, Australia, Japan

Cover: Foto ©Andreas Hilbeck / pixelio.de

More available books at **www.hansebooks.com**

THE
Stranger's Guide
IN
Baltimore and its Environs.

Sketches of Public Buildings, Monuments, Notable
Localities, Resorts, Suburban Drives, &c.

Showing Strangers where to Go and what to See.

The Centennial Exposition, Philadelphia, and Public
Buildings, Washington, &c.

————

BALTIMORE:

PUBLISHED BY JOHN MURPHY & CO.

182 BALTIMORE STREET.

BALTIMORE NEWS COMPANY.

For Sale by all Booksellers, News Dealers, &c.

1876.

INTRODUCTION.

In the pages of this Guide Book the Tourist or Sojourner is furnished with brief and accurate descriptions of the City of Baltimore, its Harbor, Shipping, Public Buildings, Historic Localities, Monuments, Libraries, Art Collections, Parks and Environs. The book gives also descriptions of all the Interesting Points within easy reach of the city, which may be visited by Rail or Water and return the same day, Showing Where to go and What to See. Among these places may be mentioned, Philadelphia and the Centennial Exposition; Washington City and the Public Buildings, Grounds and Art Galleries; Georgetown, D. C., and its charming heights; Alexandria, Va., and the Potomac river; Mt. Vernon and the Tomb of Washington; Annapolis, the United States Naval Academy and the Historical Chambers and Portraits of the State Capitol. Besides these, Routes are given of the Chesapeake Bay to Fortress Monroe, Norfolk, Old Point Comfort, the Eastern Shore of Maryland, &c.

Many interesting Statistics are given showing the great Progress of Baltimore within the past ten years, its Commercial strides, Growth and Embellishment, all combining to make it a great Metropolitan City, in the strict sense of the word, a city of Wealth, Culture and Refinement.

With the view of embodying in the most compact form, and giving all the necessary information at the lowest price Pictorial Illustrations, so generally used in such publications, are purposely omitted, and in their place, accurate descriptions and valuable details are supplied.

CONTENTS.

The Stranger's Guide in Baltimore.

Baltimore City.

The City of Baltimore was first laid out in 1730, on a tract of sixty acres of land, and in 1796, was incorporated as a town. Within the present boundaries are 12½ square miles of land and 2 of water. From east to west the boundaries are five miles apart, and from north to south four miles. Baltimore street, the chief thoroughfare, running east and west, is a little over four miles long, and is the dividing line for numbering houses on streets running north and south, while Jones' Falls, a small stream in the centre of the city, is the dividing line for numbering the houses east and west. The elevations are 0 to 250 feet above the sea level; mean annual temperature 55°; annual rainfall 44.48, and situation 39° 17' N. latitude 76° 37' longitude W.

Baltimore, though not the capital of Maryland, is the chief city of the State, and the largest emporium of the south. It is by reason of its geographical situation, on the Atlantic coast near the Chesapeake bay, as well as by its railroad connections with the great west and the south, the entreport of a large portion of the richest producing territory of the union, and the most convenient point of export for grain, flour, petroleum, cotton, tobacco and other great staples of the interior.

2   5

The striking characteristics of the city are its bright-ness, clearness of sky, blue water, active harbor, com-mercial rather than mechanical pursuits, numerous churches and homelike and hospitable traits of its peo-ple. An aspect of cheerful elegance pervades the city, which is particularly noticed by strangers. There is an absence of crowded tenements, a great number of small dwellings, where each family may have a sepa-rate home. Since 1865 upwards of 15,000 houses have been built, extending mostly over the north-western boundary and closing around Druid Hill Park, and crowning some of the highest elevations, 190 to 220 feet above tide water. Horse railways and street cars connect the city and its suburbs, and afford rapid and convenient modes of reaching any and every desired point.

The brightness of Baltimore is especially a character-istic of the north-western section, covering several square miles, built for the most part since 1865. In this region, the tall spires of numerous white marble churches tower above the lines of bright red brick dwellings. Public squares, provided with walks and seats, shade trees, grass plots, and springs of limpid water, are plentifully scattered throughout the city. Several of these squares are without enclosure, and it is an indication of the order and decorum of the inhabitants that flowers grow unmolested in the open air, and add their fragrance and beauty to the other attractions of the city's public resorts.

Among the more attractive of these green spots in the northwest, may be mentioned Lafayette and Harlem Squares; in the west, Franklin and Union Squares; in the northeast, Madison Square. For South Baltimore

Riverside Park, is this year being laid off and improved. Broadway in the east, and Eutaw Place northwest, are broad and beautiful avenues, parked in the centre with grass and adorned with flower-beds, vases with trailing vines, and growing plants.

One arm of the Patapsco river stretches far into the business centre, affording highly prized commercial facilities, and an inner harbor known as the "Basin," for passenger steamboats and coastwise and bay craft in great numbers. The channels leading to the harbor are kept at a depth of 25 feet and 200 to 300 feet wide. The deep water of the harbor, where the larger foreign and other vessels lie, is at Fells' Point and Canton on the north side, and Locust Point on the south side, above Fort McHenry. The entrance to the harbor, between Fort McHenry and the Lazaretto Lighthouse Point is narrow, but inside the river widens beautifully, and in the busy seasons presents a scene of great activity.

THE POPULATION, by municipal census in 1873, the latest taken, was 302,893, of which the female excess was 15,723. It is estimated that 50,000 of the inhabitants are of German origin. Besides the city proper, there are numerous suburban villages and hamlets, the outgrowth of overflowing population, not enumerated in the census of Baltimore. If the surrounding belt of country and these villages were annexed as contemplated, the number of inhabitants would be carried up to about 400,000, and give the city an area of nearly sixty square miles.

Commerce and Manufactures.

The value of exports and imports for the last three years were as follows:

Exports, 1875, $27,135,038   Imports, 1875, $29,790,821
"   1874, 27,524,835   "   1874, 26,578,554
"   1873, 22,387,812   "   1873, 31,319,033

The Petroleum exports were: 1875, 24,828,124 galls.; 1874, 8,381,903 galls.; 1873, 3,470,995 galls.

The value of Coffee imports was, in 1875, $13,730,020; in 1874, $9,164,667; in 1873, $10,375,413.

The total Grain receipts in 1875 were 15,028,854 bushels; in 1874, 17,086,645 bushels.

Flour receipts, 1875, 1,391,843 bbls.; in 1874, 1,560,997.

Maryland and Ohio Tobacco shipments were, in 1875, 34,366 hhds.; 1874, 51,248 hhds.; 1873, 51,652 hhds.

The total Tobacco inspections in the three years were: 1875, 40,436 hhds.; in 1874, 57.955 hhds.; and in 1873, 65,067 hhds.

The Oyster and Fruit Trade. Among leading industries, the Oyster trade occupies an important place. On Fells Point, and in South Baltimore, whole streets are occupied with Oyster and Fruit Packing establishments. Eight hundred or a thousand schooners are engaged seven months in a year in the oyster trade, and a large fleet of bay craft, to say nothing of steamers, is employed in bringing fruit and vegetables to the packing houses. In summer oysters packed in ice are shipped West, North and South. The oyster fleet, between seasons engages in other traffic especially with the West Indies, from which pine apples and other tropical fruits are brought to market and for packing. There are one hundred oyster and fruit packing firms in Baltimore, some of which have establishments at convenient localities on the bay or in the fruit growing region of the Eastern Shore. In connection with the packing business, the manufacture of tin cans is a great industry of itself. The capital employed in the different branches of the trade aggregates many millions of dollars.

The Shoe and Leather Trade of Baltimore is another of its largest industries. In 1870 the sale of Eastern and Baltimore manufactured shoes amounted to $11,000,000. In 1874 the sales were $17,000,000. There are thirty large shoe factories in the city, using improved machinery and employing 4,500 operatives. There are thirty jobbing, commission and auction houses, and the leather dealers and tanners produce the best sole leather made anywhere, as evidenced by the Vienna award to a Baltimore house engaged in this manufacture.

The statistics of the shoe and leather trade for 1874 show the following figures:

Sales of boots and shoes, wholesale and retail, .	$ 8,000,000
Manufacturers, ...	7,000,000
Rubber boots and shoes, ...	1,900,000
Auction sales, ...	750,000
Sales of leather, ...	4,000,000
Sales of hides, ...	1,375,000
Kip and calfskins and upper leather, . .	450,000
Goat skins and morocco, ...	250,000
Sheep skins, ...	150,000
Total boots, shoes and leather, . .	$22,975,000

Pianos, &c. In the manufacture of Pianos, several thousand workmen are employed. Upwards of 2,500

2*

pianos are turned out every year from the workshops. Several Organ factories have given celebrity to Baltimore made church organs.

Bell Casting is one of the best known industries. The specimens of bells sent from Baltimore foundries, to all parts of the country, speak for themselves.

Iron Manufactures. Ship building, Iron Bridge, Architectural Iron Work, extensive Railroad Foundries and Car shops at Mt. Clare and other localties owned by the Baltimore and Ohio and Northern Central Railway; *Brick Making, Tobacco Manufacture,* and many other industries too numerous to mention, are all tending by the multitude and value of their productions to give importance to the city as a manufacturing centre.

Railroad Tunnels.

By the expenditure of nearly five millions of dollars a system of underground communication has been constructed, by which all the railroads, other than the Baltimore and Ohio, are connected and brought to tide-water at Canton. This system comprises the Baltimore and Potomac and the Union Railroad Tunnels on the north side of the city.

The Baltimore and Potomac Tunnel is, with the exception of the Hoosac Tunnel, the largest on this side of the Atlantic. It was begun in 1871 and finished in 1873. The arch is built of five rings of brick, backed up with rubble masonry, and is 22 feet in height by 27 feet in width. The cost of the work was $2,300,000; length of tunnel 6,969 feet. The western entrance is at Gilmor street, and the tunnel extends throughout the city in a northeasterly direction, passing under the beds of twenty-nine streets until it emerges at North avenue, the northern boundary of the city, close to the line of the Northern Central Railway. Of this distance, 1,057 feet were worked entirely under ground at a depth of from 50 to 25 feet.

The Union Tunnel extends from Greenmount avenue on the west under thirteen streets. It is also built of brick; 3,410 feet in length, and otherwise of nearly the same dimensions as the Potomac Tunnel, of which it is practically a continuation. Both works were prosecuted simultaneously, forming the links to tide-water by double tracks through the tunnels and some open cuts. The Union Railroad, on emerging from the eastern portal, passes over two avenues on iron bridges, and then curves to the south to Canton. At a distance of three and a half miles from Greenmount avenue, the Union road makes a junction at Bay View Station with the Philadelphia, Wilmington and Baltimore line.

The roads using the tunnels are the Western Maryland, Baltimore and Potomac, Northern Central, and Philadelphia, Wilmington and Baltimore. Through trains from New York to Washington switch off from the Philadelphia, Wilmington and Baltimore to the Union Railroad, passing through the Union tunnel and over the tracks of the Northern Central; thence through the Baltimore and Potomac tunnel and over that railroad to Washington without change of cars.

New York passengers to Washington via Baltimore and Ohio Railroad are brought into the President Street Depot, of the Philadelphia, Wilmington & Baltimore Railroad and the cars are drawn through Pratt street by horses to Camden Depot, proceeding via Washington Branch to Washington.

The Railroad Depots on the north side of the city are Calvert Station; Union Depot, Charles Street; and Pennsylvania Avenue Station. The connections north and south are with the Pennsylvania Railroad. The Western Maryland Railroad which enjoys Tide Water and Tunnel facilities in common with other north side roads, has its depot, a newly constructed brick building, at the corner of Hillen and Exeter streets.

Terminal Facilities.

Locust Point is conspicuous as the terminal tide-water outlet for grain, coal, iron and other freights of the Baltimore and Ohio Railroad, as well as the site of the European Steamship piers. Federal Hill, at the junction with the main land, and Fort McHenry, at the extremity of the point, are old landmarks. Between these two, especially on the water front opposite the city, are located a great number of coal piers, by means of which the cars are emptied directly into vessels for shipment of Maryland and West Virginia bituminous coal; second, two immense Elevators, which receive the grain from the railroad, and deliver to vessels of the largest size at the elevator wharves; third, European steamship piers, active with freight all the year round, and especially busy during the summer, when the tide of tourist travel is at its height. This Point and the piers are reached by the ferry at the foot of Broadway and Thames street.

The elevators handle annually an immense quantity of grain brought from the West. Elevator A, has the capacity of nearly 600,000 bushels. The building, 80 by 150 feet, is built on 4,400 piles.

Elevator B, a few hundred feet to the east, rests upon 11,750 piles. The foundation is granite laid in cement. The building is 97 by 324 feet, and 169 feet high, capacity is 1,500,000 bushels. It is said to be impossible to discharge car loads into the elevators faster than the grain can be carried to the bins, and the only delay in loading vessels is occasioned by the necessity of stopping at intervals to properly distribute the cargo.

A railroad ferry is located between the two elevators by which trains of loaded cars are conveyed across the water to the Canton side, on immense barges to connect with the Philadelphia, Wilmington and Baltimore Railroad. During busy seasons 250 cars are transferred a day at this point.

What with present and contemplated building, the whole peninsula constitutes the scene of the most active and energetic business progress of Baltimore, and it is thought will soon root out Fort McHenry as a military depot, and replace its barracks and arsenals with the warehouse and granaries of commerce.

Oil Yards. On the other side of the peninsula, fronting on the Middle branch of the Patapsco, are established oil yards and depots doing an immense business. The cars bring the oil from Pennsylvania and West Virginia directly to the water's edge, where there is a fleet of foreign vessels ready to receive cargoes. The oil yards are quite as well worth a visit as the steamship piers and grain elevators.

Canton, a thriving manufacturing and commercial town of itself, forms the eastern extremity of Baltimore opposite Fort McHenry.

The Canton Company here owns 2,800 acres of land, comprising 18,000 building lots. Streets are laid out and paved. The water frontage is about 20,000 feet, on water ranging from fifteen to twenty-five feet deep. Upwards of sixty manufactories are congregated within the area of Canton, employing about 8,000 hands. These factories include Oyster and Fruit Packing Houses, Stove and Hollow Ware Foundries, Copper Works, Rolling Mill, Chemical and Fertilizing Factories, eight Coal Oil Refineries, Copper Smelting Furnaces, Car Wheel, Agricultural Implement, White Lead and other factories; Lager Beer Breweries and Distilleries.

The Copper Works are very extensive and promise in time to rank among the leading industries of Baltimore. The Canton Elevator, and terminal facilities of the Union Railroad, are also conspicuous features.

An extensive coal pier, large wharves, warehouses, furnish terminal facilities to meet existing requirements, with prospective extensions in several directions. One of the great features of Canton is the extensive rolling mill which turns out immense quantities of steel and iron rails. In busy seasons very many of the largest vessels lie at the wharves of Canton.

Historical Localities.

Federal Hill. From this notable point a good view of Baltimore is commanded. It is also the site of the Marine Observatory, from which marine arrivals are signalled. Federal Hill is so called from having been the point in 1788 that the news of the adoption of the Federal Constitution by the Virginia Convention was proclaimed by artillery. This hill will be converted into a public park, for which purpose it has been purchased by the city at a cost of $64,000.

Fort McHenry possesses national historic interest as the scene of the bombardment in 1814 when the British land and naval forces were repulsed in their attack on Baltimore. It was during this bombardment that Francis S. Key, a prisoner on a British vessel off the fort, wrote the Star Spangled Banner which was published and sung publicly in Baltimore a few days afterwards, and soon became the national air. Fort McHenry, originally a brick fort, has in later years been greatly improved and strengthened by earthworks. It is now provided with extensive modern barracks, heavy guns, and garrisoned by several companies of artillery. The grounds are large and handsome. Every Sunday evening in warm weather the band plays and the public is admitted to the open air concerts. The fort is reached by the Ferry at the foot of Broadway, and is half a mile from the Ferry landing on the Locust Point side.

One historical incident may be not out of place in connection with historical places this centennial year. In December, 1776, on the approach of the royal troops toward the Delaware, the Continental Congress adjourned from Philadelphia to Baltimore. The Congress met in Baltimore Dec. 20th, 1776. They met and continued in session in a spacious three-story and attic brick building which stood until a few years since on the south side of Baltimore street, from Sharp to Liberty street, now covered with extensive business establishments. The house belonged to Jacob Fite, and was at the time the farthest house west in the town and one of the largest; while Washington was achieving the victory at Trenton, Congress was sitting in Baltimore and taking measures to strengthen his hands. It was here that Gen. Gates came to confer with Congress, and on the 27th of December, 1776, before the Congress in Baltimore could have learned of the victory at Trenton, Gen. Washington was vested by an act passed in this city with supreme power for raising troops, munitions and subsistence stores, &c , in all respects constituting him a dictator in the old Roman sense of the term.   It was in Maryland, too, in the Senate Chamber at Annapolis, that after achieving the Independence of his country, he resigned his commission and laid down the supreme power conferred upon him at Baltimore.

Fort Carroll, an unfinished granite work rising from the middle of the Patapsco about 6 miles below the city, is a fortification on the plan of Fort Sumter, Charleston Harbor, S. C., and of a class of military structures practically useless against modern ordnance. Work on Fort Carroll has been abandoned some years. Visitors are not permitted to land and the work is in charge of a Sergeant with a light keeper for the lighthouse.   A number of heavy guns are in the casemates.

Quarantine Grounds and the Marine Hospital are located on the south side below Fort McHenry. Visiting not allowed.

Prominent Buildings.

The City Hall of Baltimore, recently erected, is a marble palace in the Renaissance style of architecture, centrally located, covering a block of ground, bounded by Fayette, North, Lexington and Holliday streets, on each of which there are entrances, the main one being on Holliday street, facing the east.   The area of the block within the building line is 35,000 square feet.   The total cost of the pile including ground and furniture was $2,271,135. It is a matter of pride among Baltimoreans, that out of an appropriation of $2,500,000 to construct the City Hall, $228,865 was surplus. Seven years were occupied in the construction of the building, and its dedication, October 25th, 1875 was among the last official acts of the Mayoralty of Hon. Joshua Vansant, chairman of the Building Committee.

The structure is four stories high, French roof with iron dome reaching 260 feet from the ground. A balcony 250 feet from the street affords a magnificent view of the city. Visitors are permitted to ascend to this balcony only on Mondays, from 10 A. M. to 3 P. M. A clock with four dials and a bell weighing 6,000 lbs. are in the dome which is 170 feet in circumference,

All the departments of the city government are gathered in the building, including the Mayor's office, City Council chambers and a large public Hall for State occasions.

The first, or ground floor is occupied by the City Commissioner, Inspector of Public Buildings, Fire Commissioners, Health Department, Water Department, Police Marshall, City Detectives.

On the second, or principal floor are the Mayor's Offices, City Register, Comptroller, Collector, Appeal Tax Court, School Board, Street Commissioners and Park Commissioners.

The third floor is occupied by the Chambers of both Branches of the City Council; the grand Public Hall, City Library, Law Offices, Water Board, City Surveyors and Engineers.

The Baltimore Safe Deposit Company's Building on South street, is considered one of the very few absolutely fire and burglar proof structures in

3

the country. Below ground it is a building within a building, and the foundations are laid below the tide water level so as to impede mining by burglars, with a flow of water. The outer walls are from three to seven feet in thickness, and the interior walls of the treasure and trunk vaults seven to nine feet thick. The front of the building, combining an appearance of Egyptian strength with Roman solidity of construction and modern grace, stamps the structure with individuality. The material is wholly of bricks, except some stone trimming of the front, and the walls are made so strong as to remain unshaken by surrounding piles falling on them, or any other assaults than from heavy ordnance.

The safe cost $78,000, and it is as strong as an iron Monitor, of massive and ornamental front thirty by twenty-five feet, and nine feet high in the clear inside, with capacity for 5,000 boxes of depositors. The material is chilled iron and steel that will resist the drill, and the weight is estimated at 500 tons.

The Shot Tower, at the corner of Front and Fayette streets has stood nearly fifty years a monument to the skill of Baltimore brick layers. The foundation stone was laid on the 4th of July, 1828, by Charles Carroll of Carrollton, who, the same day laid the foundation stone of the Baltimore and Ohio railroad. The walls were built from scaffolding on the inside, and are six feet thick at the base and two feet thick at the top. From the pavement, the structure rises 216 feet; its circumference at the base is 180 feet and 51 feet at the top.

Alexandrowski, the city residence of Mr. Thos. Winans, surrounded by a wall and located on Baltimore, Fremont and Hollins streets, is one of the notable private city residences with ornamental grounds. Ad-

joining the mansion is a Music hall, in which Mr.
Winans has built a large organ on new principles. A
tall chimney, towering above everything in the grounds,
is part of a system of ventilation, in which valuable
and practical results have been reached. The "Cigar
Steamer," with which Mr. Winans' name has long been
associated, lies at the wharf of his shipyard, Ferry Bar,
South Baltimore, where the Patapsco Navy Regatta
Clubs have their boat houses. The locality is reached
by the South Baltimore Blue cars.

The Young Men's Christian Association
Building, N. W. corner Charles and Saratoga streets, is
one of the most prominent buildings erected within the
past few years. It is of brick, with Ohio sandstone
trimmings, and is a lofty, commodious structure. The
halls, reading, recreation and business rooms are on
magnificent scale, and calculated to rank the structure,
when finished, with any similar building in any other
of the larger cities. The Association has branches in all
the large towns of the State.

The Young Men's Catholic Association
have their rooms and Library at the S. E. corner of
Charles and Lexington streets. They are taking steps
for the erection of a fine building for their purposes.

Bayview Asylum—the almshouse—is a very note-
worthy building. It is appropriately named on account
of its magnificent situation and the charming view of the
Chesapeake Bay to be had from its site. The situation
is indeed most conspicuous, for it is the first object seen
in approaching the harbor, and is in sight from every
other point of observation in and around the city. It is
a large brick pile with a dome rising from the central
building, and is the home of about 650 paupers.

Monuments.

The Washington Monument. Baltimore has merited the title of "the Monumental City," chiefly by its simple and beautiful doric column to the "Father of his Country," which, when built between the years 1815 and 1830, stood alone a towering shaft in the midst of a noble wood, on land formerly belonging to the country seat of General John Eager Howard, and known as Howard's Park.   Now the monument is in the centre of Mt. Vernon Place, one of the most beautiful localities in any city of America.   The Washington Monument was "erected to George Washington by the State of Maryland."   It is surmounted by a statue of Washington, 16 feet high, and the whole stands 212 feet from the ground, and 280 feet above tide water. From the top, to which visitors are permitted to ascend, a beautiful view of the city may be had

From the four sides of the square base of the column, grass plats radiate north, south, east and west, in the centre of Monument and Charles streets, from the intersection of which the shaft rises beautifully.   Mt. Vernon Place is a collection of magnificent dwellings, and the architectural effect of the surroundings is striking.   Few American or European cities can boast of a more beautiful locality.

Battle Monument, erected by the city to the memory of the citizens who fell in defense of Baltimore in the war with Great Britain.   It is in the centre of the city, at the head of what is known as Monument Square, (Calvert street,) in which town meetings are held.   The Court House and several large hotels are in the immediate vicinity and a hack stand is conveniently near. The structure is 52 feet high and is of beautiful design, intended to be allegorical. The shaft surmounting the monumental structure is in the form of fasces to represent strength and union. Lachrymal urns indicate the purpose of the monument, and the names of those who lost their lives are inscribed on the entablature. The whole is crowned by a female figure representing the City of Baltimore, having a wreath of laurel in one hand uplifted.

Wells and McComas Monument. Another monument commemorative of an incident of the repulse of the British at North Point in the land attack, September 12th, 1814, is located at Ashland Square, formed by the intersection of Monument, Aisquith, and Gay streets. This tribute is to the memory of two youths, Wells and McComas who are said to have killed the British General Ross leading the attack. Their bones were exhumed and deposited in the Square in 1858. In 1871 the monument was erected. It is a simple marble obelisk on a square die block and pedestal, the whole about 30 feet high.

Odd Fellows' Memorial. On Broadway, in the eastern section of the city, a monument stands, erected by the Odd Fellows to Thomas Wildey, a native of England who introduced the order into the United States and is regarded as the founder in this country. He established the first lodge in Baltimore in 1819. The monument was erected in 1865, a few years after his death. It is a Grecian Doric column rising from a singular pedestal, the whole 52 feet high. The figure of a woman and children surmount the column.

The Poe Monument. The last and the least of the monuments of the city, is that erected in 1875 by

3*

the Public Schools of Baltimore, to Edgar Allan Poe, the poet whose remains are buried in the Westminster Presbyterian Church yard, corner of Greene and Fayette streets. The monument is simply a pedestal or die block, with an ornamental cap, wholly of marble, resting on two marble slabs and a granite base. A medallion portrait of the poet by the sculptor Volck is chiselled on the front of the die block, and the inscription is simply

"Edgar Allan Poe: born Jan'y 20, 1819; died Oct. 7, 1849."

Public Parks.

Druid Hill Park. The Parks of Baltimore, as well as the Public Squares, are noted for their quiet beauty. Druid Hill Park, about two and a half miles from the centre of the city, is a Park in the true sense of the word, having herds of Deer ranging its thick green woods, and flocks of Sheep feeding on grassy hillsides, adding pastoral beauty to the broad meadows. No one who will ride through the beautiful drives of Druid Hill Park, or stroll through its sunny lawns or quiet dells or climb its wooded hills, or rest in the shady spots where Springs murmur, can fail to be impressed or delighted with the beauty nature has lavished on the spot. Art is not needed for embellishment. The few structures required are generally well placed and harmonize with the natural surroundings.

The main approach from Madison avenue is a broad way through a Stone Gateway. Beyond the entrance is Swann Avenue, flanked with large Urns on Pedestals, from which, in summer time, trailing vines hang and a variety of flowers grow. To the right is a Drive fifty feet wide and a mile and a half in length around

Druid Lake, belonging to the City Water Works. From a white Moorish Tower at the southeast corner of this lake, there is a beautiful Bay view overlooking the city, and immediately below, at the base of the hill is Mount Royal avenue, another main approach from the city. Mount Royal Reservoir, close at hand, sends forth a feathery plume from its fountain, while a Jet near the western end of Druid Lake sends up a stream 90 to 100 feet high through a five-inch nozzle, forming, when playing, one of the grandest fountains to be seen anywhere.

Passing from the northern extremity of Swann avenue through the shady walks of a delightful stretch of woods to the Grand Promenade, which embellishes a Central portion of the Park, a splendid Landscape opens to the view. On both sides of the promenade is a grassy demesne, dotted with trees and merging here and there into woodland, while at the end of the promenade stands a Turkish Kiosk, encircled by statues half hidden in shrubbery, and planted boldly against a back ground of forest and hill scenery.

Towards the centre of the grounds is the " Mansion House," open in the summer for Refreshments. A broad piazza runs all around the house, affording seats for rest and observation. The cupola permits a glimpse of the bay. Fountains play in front, and a short distance beyond is a Lake, sometimes crowded with merry parties of rowers, and in winter with skaters.

In the rear of the Mansion is a beautiful walk through a long valley, in which is a Pavilion containing the nucleus of a Zoological Collection. Garrett's bridge is in one of the most picturesque spots in the Park. Near it is the Fish Hatching House, where Food

Fishes in all the stages of Hatching are exposed for Public Instruction.

In the north-western part of the Park, is the High Service Reservoir for supplying the highest city elevations with water, pumped from the Pump House near Druid Lake through underground mains into the receptacle and thence distributed.

One of the most interesting spots in Druid Hill is the locality known as Tempest Hill, overlooking the valley of Jones' Falls and the Manufacturing village of Woodberry, where Poole & Hunt have their Extensive Machine Shops, and Cotton Duck and other Cotton Mills give employment to several thousand operatives. Woodberry contains a thrifty population and is a collection of neat cottages and industrious inhabitants. North of this portion of the Park is spread out before the observer a rich and beautiful rolling country under cultivation.

Seats are provided in all the choice spots of the Park, where the weary may rest or where the eyes of observers may delight to dwell on views and objects of interest. The numerous springs have ornamental structures and statuary, generally contributed by liberal and public spirited citizens. In some of the Glades, oaks 15 feet in circumference shade the choicest resting places, and the woods generally are of fine old trees that would ennoble any park.

Druid Hill contains with additions 700 acres. Originally it was 475 acres, costing in 1858, $1,000 an acre. The frontage on the east side is an unbroken line along the Northern Central Railway and the valley of Jones' Falls is a mile and a quarter.

Druid Hill Park is reached from the city by Madison avenue and Pennsylvania avenue street cars, Citizen's

Line cars, Northern Central Railway Steam cars, from Calvert Depot in the city to Woodberry Station, and Reisterstown road Horse cars. At Mt. Royal avenue and Madison avenue entrances, Park carriages convey visitors through the different drives and to all the points of interest. Horse cars from Boundary avenue, near the city street car termini, also carry passengers to the Park station near the Mansion.

Patterson Park, in the eastern section of the city, contains some fifty-one acres of Land. It is a great popular resort, and in respect to the fine view it affords of the Harbor, River and Bay, is one of the most attractive spots in the city. The Water view is its distinguishing charm. Here one may sit all the long summer afternoon under shade, and see the vessels come in and go out between the Lazaretto Light House and Fort McHenry at the Harbor's entrance, and beyond eight miles down Fort Carroll in the centre of the river, and still further beyond North Point Light House and the Bay, dotted with sails.

Strictly speaking the ground is not a Park. The trees are few and generally small, affording but little shade, except from a few Catalpas. Judicious Gardening and engineering, however, have given the spot distinctive characteristics, and the work of improvement is continuous. On summer afternoons thousands of children play on the green grass and the lawns are covered with croquet parties. There is a Boating Lake; a Conservatory newly erected after an ornamental design, Swings and Dancing Pavilion, and a beautiful Mall. Seats are provided in great numbers, but scarcely sufficient at all times to meet the wants of the crowds of people who visit the Park. A Playing Fountain, the

Basin of which is filled with Gold Fish, stands opposite the main entrance. The Citizens Line of street cars pass the great gate.

Water Works.

Until the Spring of 1874, the source of the water supply of Baltimore city was Jones' Falls and a few small tributaries, gathered at Lake Roland, and thence conveyed to storage reservoirs and distributed. The capacity of Jones' Falls in dry seasons is 15,000,000 gallons daily. This came to be much below the needs of the city, and a temporary supply equal to 10,000,000 gallons daily was obtained by a pump at Meredith's Ford on the Gunpowder river, and increasing the flow of Roland Run to Lake Roland.

Now a permanent supply from the Gunpowder is added to the system of water works. A dam will be erected on the Gunpowder river a short distance above Mine Bank Run, and a lake thus formed will extend up the river as far as Meredith's Ford Bridge, at the Dulaney's Valley turnpike, where the pump house, connected with the "Temporary Supply" is located. From this lake, at the dam, the water will be brought by natural flow through a straight conduit of 12 feet internal diameter, and having a capacity of 170,000,000 gallons per day, to the main distributing Lake or reservoir This Lake, or reservoir, is located back of Montebello, between the Hillen and Harford roads, in a natural basin formed by one of the tributaries of Herring Run. Its water area will be about 80 acres and the surface elevation will be 160 feet above mean tide; its storage capacity, 700,000,000 gallons. The conduit will be continued of the same size from Lake Montebello, to a point on the

Harford road opposite Homestead, whence pipes will be laid to connect with the City pipe system at North Boundary avenue and Washington street.

At present water is brought from Lake Roland four miles by a brick aqueduct underground, along the Falls road to Hampden Reservoir; thence by two large mains through the Stop House into Druid Lake. A third main from Hampden passes through the Pump House, Druid Hill Park, into Druid Lake and is tapped for the High Service Reservoir in the Park.

Druid Lake is the great distributing body of water. Mt. Royal, connected with Druid Lake by Mt. Royal avenue, is 16 feet lower than Druid Lake, and is the distributing reservoir for the lower section of the City. Hampden Reservoir is simply the feeder for Druid Lake, but can be made a supply reservoir. The High Service Reservoir in Druid Hill Park is 350 feet above tide and distributes three millions of gallons daily to the highest elevations.

Druid Lake is one mile and a half around; the embankment is 60 feet thick at the top and 600 feet at the base; the greatest depth of water is 65 feet and from that to 20 feet.

The storage capacity of reservoirs, &c., in present use is as follows: Lake Roland, 300,000,000 gallons; Hampden, 46,000,000; Conduit, 6,000,000; Druid Lake, 520,000,000; Mt. Royal, 30,000,000; High Service Reservoir, 27,000,000; Total, 938,000,000 gallons.

Utilizing Druid Hill Park with a part of the system of water works adds interesting features to the otherwise charming locality. Lakes Roland and Montebello can be reached in an afternoon's drive, and their situations in delightful and picturesque neighborhoods will well repay visitation.

Elevations Above Tide.

LOCALITIES.	FEET.	LOCALITIES.	FEET.
Patterson Park, . . .	125	Baltimore & Gilmor, . .	112
Maryland Institute, . .	5	" " Payson,	186
Gay and Aisquith, . .	39	Richmond Market, . .	124
Penitentiary Gate, . .	52	Washington Monument,	98
Leadenhall & Stockholm		Eutaw and Madison, .	122
sts., South Baltimore,	3	Fayette and Fulton, . .	155
Federal Hill, ...	85	Gilmor and Presbury, .	213
Baltimore & Light, . .	68	Woodyear & Presstman,	205
" " Fremont, .	65	Druid Hill Park, highest,	360
" " Republican,	88		

Cemeteries.

THE Principal Cemeteries of Baltimore are Greenmount, on the York road; Baltimore Cemetery, on the Belair road; Mount Olivet, Western and Loudoun Park, on the Catonsville road, and Mt. Carmel on the Trappe road.

Greenmount. One of the distinguishing natural features of Greenmount is the Beautiful Mound from which it takes its name, crowned with an Ornamental Brown Stone Gothic Chapel. The lots are laid out with stone curbing. A beautiful diversity of hill and dale, valley and grove, affords a good basis for ornamentation; but there are parts of the Cemetery already too much crowded with glaring white marble. A gray granite Mansoleum of Egyptian style of Architecture is in the Centre of the grounds. In the great congregation of monuments two works of Rinehart, the Maryland sculptor, whose remains repose ¸in the Cemetery, are conspicuous. One of these works is a Bronze Female Figure above life size, standing on a granite pedestal, dropping Memorial Flowers ; the other represents two Sleeping Children in marble. Both are works of genius. In all parts of the grounds the names of the noted dead of Baltimore may be seen—among them, Reverdy Johnson, Major Ringgold of Mexican War fame, and hundreds of others. On one of the Hills in the southern part of the grounds is a large Monument and Statue by the City of Baltimore to John McDonogh, who bequeathed to the city a large estate for educational purposes.

Among the noted monuments is that of the Elder Booth the great tragedian, close to which, without any stone to designate it, is the ivy-covered grave of John Wilkes Booth. Tickets of admission are required of all who are not lot holders, and may be had at No. 53 Lexington street. The York road cars convey passengers within thirty feet of the main entrance and wicket. To the west of this is the Institution for the Blind.

Baltimore Cemetery is reached by the Gay street Red Line of cars. This burial place is at the northeastern boundary of the city on an elevated situation. The Office of the Cemetery is at No. 8 South street.

Mount Olivet Cemetery is situate about 2 miles west of the city on the Frederick road, and from its elevated position commands an excellent view of the city and bay.

Western Cemetery is located about 1½ miles west of the city on the margin of Gwynn's Falls, and is reached by way of West Baltimore street extended.

4

Loudoun Park Cemetery is three miles from Baltimore, reached by the Catonsville horse cars. The grounds are well wooded with large trees, laid out in drives, and affords some magnificent views of the city harbor, bay, and the charming valley between the city and the Cemetery. In Loudoun Park are interred the remains of Confederate Soldiers, transferred from distant battle fields of Gettysburg, Antietam, &c., or who died in Prison. A commemorative Statue occupies the centre of the rows of dead. The remains of 1,646 Union Soldiers are also interred in a Reservation in another part of the Cemetery. Both spots are on "Memorial Days" the scene of the annual ceremony of Strewing Flowers, &c. Two of Rinehart's works in marble are among the notable Monuments of Loudoun Park, representing the Scriptural Declaration: "I am the Resurrection and the Life." The Office of the Cemetery is No. 19½ South street.

The New Cathedral Cemetery, (Bonny Brae,) is located on the Old Frederick road. From the western part of this Cemetery one of the best views of the city may be had. The Cemetery is beautifully laid out.

Suburban Drives.

THE ridges of hills surrounding Baltimore shelter the city, and with the influence of the water combine to give it the ·fine climate which is its characteristic. Numerous delightful drives on excellent roads may be found in every direction.

On the eastward, Shell Roads are much used for pleasure driving. Numerous Pavilions and Excursion Grounds as far down as North Point, and what is called

" the Neck " attract pleasure seekers and fishing parties.
The Philadelphia road East Fayette street extended,
leads to Herring Run Trotting Course.

North Point Battle-field is a pleasant ride from Baltimore via Philadelphia road, turning out on the Trappe
road southwardly. North Point by land is fifteen miles
from Baltimore. At the Monument House Inn, seven
miles down, is a small monument erected to the memory
of those who fell in defense of Baltimore in 1814. Near
Numsen's Gate, a large tree is shown under which the
British General Ross was killed by the youths, Wells
and McComas.

On the north-east, the Harford road, Aisquith
street extended, leading to Belair through suburban villages and a thickly settled and beautiful stretch of country. One of the largest and finest estates on the road
is Clifton, belonging to the Johns Hopkins University
and formerly the country seat of the founder. Montebello the large estate of John W. Garrett is opposite
Clifton and extends along the Hillen road. Horse cars
run on the Harford road from the City Hall and North
street to Darley Park Pleasure Grounds and to Hall's
Springs, three and a half miles, a popular resort.

Gay street extended is also a road to Belair, Harford county. The Red Line street cars pass a number
of Breweries, Beer Gardens and Pleasure Resorts of
German citizens. Among the chief of these resorts is
the Schuetzen Park, which possesses Shooting Ranges,
Bowling Alleys and other amusements.

The York Road, due north to Towsontown, the
County Seat of Baltimore county, seven miles, is almost
a continuous village. Horse cars leave the corner of
Holliday and Baltimore streets. On the line are some

of the finest country seats in Maryland, including Guildford, the splendid estate of Mr. A. S. Abell, two miles from the city limits, extending westwardly from the York road to Charles street avenue. The trip on one of the "Double-Deck" cars affords a view of Waverly, Homewood, and Govanstown villages near by, and a country thickly dotted with villas, stately mansions, wooded hills, and cultivated fields. The rise of the ground is steady and a Bay view may be had from the road. Towsontown has two good Hotels and numerous Summer Boarding Houses.

Charles street avenue on the north, is a fashionable drive. This road, running nearly parallel with the York road is a broad avenue, and has in sight many manors and fine estates. Notre Dame Convent and School, is one of the most commanding situations near Baltimore, three miles from the city, and the Shepherd Asylum near Towsontown are among the most conspicuous buildings. The estates of Samuel H. Adams, David M. Perine, William H. Perot, and others, are among the finest country seats on the Charles street avenue.

On the north-west, where Pennsylvania avenue and Madison avenue street cars converge, Pimlico and Pikesville Horse cars continue on to Pimlico Race Course. Here the Maryland Jockey Club Spring and Fall Meetings are Turf events. The country is high and Pimlico is on a broad plateau. The Race Course is improved by a fine Club House, Grand Stand, extensive Stables, and other structures for the combined purposes of Agricultural Exhibitions and Jockey Club Meetings. The Reisterstown road leads to Pikesville and the old United States Arsenal.

The Falls Road. Along the valley of Jones' Falls, on what is known as the Falls road, are many attractive spots. The road passes near Woodberry, Hampden village and Reservoir, along the covered conduit line east of Mount Washington to Lake Roland. The two latter places, comprising charming and delightful views, are among the most interesting of Baltimore suburban localities, and are reached by the Northern Central Railway.

Mount Washington is laid out regularly along the slope and summit of the ridge facing the east. Its elevation, purity of air and accessibility from the city make it a charming Summer residence and temporary resort. It is also the seat of some fine Schools for young ladies.

Highland Park, a suburb of handsome villas on regularly laid out avenues, commands a sweeping and magnificent view of the Bay and the intervening city. This elevation is one of the highest, close to the city. It is reached by driving out Franklin street west, or by the Baltimore, Calverton and Powhattan Horse cars. Highland Park Hotel, open in Summer, is furnished in a style of great elegance.

The Franklin road, in this neighborhood, is a delightful drive in view of some fine estates, including the Crimea, belonging to Mr. Thomas Winans.

Windsor Heights, on the Old Windsor Mill road, is a delightful locality reached by the Calverton and Powhattan horse railway.

The village of Franklin and the Western suburbs may be reached by horse cars from the Western terminus of the Red line of street cars.

The Catonsville Horse cars carry passengers from West Baltimore street extended, to Catonsville and Elli

. 4*

cott city. The ride is in view of numerous summer residences, villages, &c. Mount De Sales, Academy for young ladies, conducted by the Sisters of the Visitation, occupies the highest point of the Catonsville range of hills, known as Hunting Ridge. The town itself is a charming summer residence with a refined and cultivated society. Mt. De Sales is probably on as great an elevation as Mt. Washington, and the school is well worth a visit. Ellicott city beyond is reached by the Baltimore and Ohio Railroad, and is the seat of some of the largest Flouring Mills in the country. It is also one of the oldest towns in Maryland. The Maryland Hospital for the Insane, Spring Grove, is near Catonsville.

Between Mt. De Sales and Baltimore lie numerous institutions, including the Passionists Monastery, opposite Loudoun Park, St Agnes' Hospital and St. Mary's Industrial School for Boys.

Calverton, close to the city, is a thriving suburb, thick with drove yards, curled hair factories and flouring mills. Gwynn's Falls is crossed by a bridge, and on the hill west of the stream is the House of Refuge, a Reformatory Institution for Boys, a massive stone pile.

Southwardly from Baltimore there are beautiful drives over Ferry Bar Bridge, across the Patapsco into Anne Arundel County. The Bridge affords a delightful Water view. The turnpike to Washington city is out Columbia street, south Baltimore.

Educational Institutions.

PUBLIC and individual contributions have for half a century been earnestly directed towards general education in the city, and Students will, in a few years, find in

Baltimore opportunities for higher cultivation not excelled by any other city on the American continent.   Already the educational institutions of Baltimore rank high. The city has in 1876 as many as 125 Public Schools, 706 teachers and 45,565 pupils, costing over $600,000 a year for maintenance.   The number of schools for colored children is fifteen, in charge of sixty-eight white teachers, and comprising 3,562 pupils.   There are six English-German Schools in which the German language is taught in connection with English branches.   These schools are among the largest in the city.

The United States sloop-of-war Juniata is at present stationed in the harbor for Nautical School purposes and training enlisted boys as seamen for the United States Naval Service.   The school is already large.

Primary, Grammar and a few Evening Schools form the basis of the system of public instruction.   At the head of these is Baltimore City College for young men, and two Female High Schools for young women. Drawing and designing is taught in all the public schools, and music to a certain extent.

Added to the public schools maintained at the city's expense are twenty or more large and flourishing Catholic Male and Female Parochial Schools, with Colleges and Academies under different Religious orders.   There are besides numerous Private Schools, Young Ladies' Seminaries, &c., which are largely patronized from the South.

For the education of Public School Teachers there is a Normal School with 147 pupils.   A Normal School for the education of Catholic Parochial School Teachers has been organized also in connection with the Institution conducted by the Sisters of the Holy Cross, near Lafayette Square.

The State Normal School Building, one of the finest structures, architecturally, in the city, is located at the northwest corner of Lafayette Square. The building is of brick and Ohio sand-stone trimmings, with a lofty spire and conspicuous slate roof. It fronts 120 feet on Carrollton avenue and 105 feet on Townsend street. The tower at the corner of the two fronts is 20 feet square at the base and rises 175 feet. The ventilation of the building is the most complete of all the many educational institutions of the city.

There are 240 pupils in attendance at the State Normal School. The number of graduates since 1865, when the School was organized, has been over 200. Each County in the State is entitled to two students for each of its representatives in the General Assembly. The law requires the appointees to be not less than 16 years of age for young women and not less than 17 years of age for young men. A limited number of other pupils are taken on payment of tuition. The main object of the School is to give professional training to those who intend to become teachers.

The Maryland Institute, for the Promotion of Mechanic Arts, is one of the older institutions of Baltimore, in the grade of special cultivation. Its objects are the general diffusion of Knowledge, and especially Instruction in the Arts. It is located on Baltimore street in the centre of the city, over the Centre Market. The building is 350 feet long by 60 wide and three stories high, fronting on Baltimore street. For a long time the Institute Hall was, and is yet to a great extent, the great popular gathering place.

The Maryland Institute has performed a noble mission in the advancement of Mechanic Arts and in the instruction of artizans. Its Library is open every day. Its departments include a School of Practical Chemistry, School of Design for males and females, an Educational Department in which women are taught Book-Keeping and to be Accountants, Music Schools which are largely attended, Public Lectures during the winter and Industrial Expositions annually until within the past year or so. New life will be infused into the exhibitions after this year, when every thing in this line is directed to the Philadelphia Centennial. The membership of the Maryland Institute in prosperous years has averaged 2,500 to 3,000 members.

The Peabody Institute at the south-east corner of Charles and Monument streets, occupies a higher plane in the scale of public education. It was founded in 1857 by George Peabody, who had the pleasure of witnessing the inauguration of his generous plans for Baltimore in common with so many broad, benevolent inspirations in other cities. The Peabody Institute is a white marble structure, containing a large Lecture and Concert Hall, Library and Offices. The Conservatory of Music and Art Gallery is now being built as part of the orginal design, on Monument street adjoining the present structure. There are four departments of the Institute, viz :

1st. LIBRARY, 58,000 volumes, chiefly standard works of reference for students and scholars. Open daily from 9 A. M. to 10 P. M. except Sundays. The Reading Room and books are free to all. Books are not allowed to be taken out.

2d. LECTURES, including the latest discoveries in science, and comprising about one hundred every year at nominal prices for the course. These lectures have heretofore covered the best fields and have been by specialists in their different departments.

3d. CONSERVATORY OF MUSIC. Instruction is given to more advanced students by a select corps of teachers as to theory and execution, vocal and instrumental at exceedingly low rates. A popular feature of this department is the orchestra of over fifty performers, and twelve or more concerts yearly for public instruction and entertainment.

4th. THE GALLERY OF ART. This department has not yet been opened. The nucleus of a collection has been formed. One of the conspicuous attractions in the Institute adjoining the reading room is a beautiful statue of Clytie by Rinehart. The Venus with shell and a bust of Pocahontas are also on exhibition. The Clytie is considered the masterpiece of Rinehart and one of the finest works of art in Baltimore. It was a gift to the Peabody Institute by Mr. John W. McCoy.

The Baltimore City College, which is the head of the city public school system has the names of 450 students on its roll for 1876, with eleven teachers or professors. The College building is on North Howard street near the Academy of Music. The structure is in what is known as the Collegiate Gothic style of architecture. Its outline is well broken and relieved; the façade is flanked on each side by a turret with a gable in the centre, relieved by a bay window on two of the three stories above the basement. A drinking fountain is placed at the base of the buttress. Entrance porches are on each side of the centre. The main tower is 110 feet high. The interior is admirably arranged for school purposes. A Free Public School Library for students and teachers has been founded in the College building.

The Schools of Medicine, &c.

The University of Maryland and *Washington University* are known throughout the country. Every year large classes of graduates receive diplomas here. Within the past few years the *College of Physicians and Surgeons* has also been added to this department of special instruction.

The Maryland University School, at the corner of Lombard and Greene streets, has been in operation many years. Connected with it is an extensive hospital.

Washington University has also a large hospital corner of Calvert and Saratoga streets.

LAW SCHOOL OF THE UNIVERSITY OF MARYLAND, 32 Mulberry street, ranks high as a Law School.

The Johns Hopkins University, endowed by a gift of over three million dollars from Johns Hopkins of Baltimore, (who died December 24th, 1873,) is now being organized and will receive its faculty and students in the autumn of 1876. Temporary class-rooms, a public lecture-room, a library and reading-room, and physical, chemical and biological laboratories, have been provided in North Howard street, near the City College and the Academy of Music. The permanent site of the University is expected to be at Clifton, the founder's estate, on the Harford road, two miles from the centre of the city. At the outset the literary and scientific faculty will be instituted; the medical and law faculties will follow later. The staff will include at first a President, eight or ten professors, ten non-resident lecturers, several associate instructors, and ten "Fellows," selected from various parts of the country. Twenty-five free scholarships have also been instituted, twenty of which are restricted to candidates from Maryland, Virginia, and North Carolina, and five are open by competition to students from any place. The foundation is free from political and ecclesiastical control.

The Johns Hopkins Hospital, founded also by a gift of over three million dollars, from Johns Hopkins, will be built on Broadway, corner of Monument street,—the selected site embracing fourteen acres. The Trustees are now elaborating the plans of the structure, having secured extended papers from five professional writers which have been published in a volume entitle " Hospital Plans." It is expected that the foundations will be laid in the autumn of 1876. The hospital, when constructed, will be for all classes of cases, except those afflicted with contagious or mental disease. In its development the Hospital will include a Dispensary, a Training School for Nurses, and a Convalescent Hospital. It will also be connected with the Medical Department of the Johns Hopkins University.

The Johns Hopkins Colored Orphan Asylum. The same benefactor has established an Orphan Asylum for three hundred colored children. The permanent site is in the western suburbs of the city, and includes 24 acres. The temporary Home is on Biddle street, where about forty orphans are now cared for.

McDonogh Foundations. Among other founders of public educational institutions who have been great benefactors of Baltimore, is John McDonogh of New Orleans, a native of Baltimore, who died in 1850, and divided his vast wealth by will between the city of his birth and that of his business career. The share to Baltimore, after the estate had undergone the vicissitudes of the late civil war and the costs of suits, amounted to

$817,000, and some lands, the value of which is not yet determined. A farm school has been established twelve miles from Baltimore, on the Western Maryland Railroad. The estate is fine and productive. The school was organized in 1873, and has a capacity for about fifty boys, who are trained to out of door labor. The school is not reformatory, and the boys are chosen from among the virtuous poor, on evidences of high character —such boys indeed as may need a lift and will afterwards have pluck enough to climb for themselves.

Free Schools.

The McKim Free School, under the direction of the Society of Friends, was founded in 1817 on bequests by John McKim. The classic granite structure, in imitation of the temple of Theseus, was built by Isaac McKim, at the corner of Baltimore and Aisquith streets, for the school. These free schools were just in advance of the public school system in Baltimore, since so largely developed. The first public school houses built by the city were at the north-east corner of Aisquith and Fayette streets, in the eastern section of the city, and at the north-eastern corner of Greene and Fayette streets, in the western section of the city.

The Oliver Hibernian Free Schools for boys and girls, on North street, near Lexington street, were founded in 1827 by bequest of John Oliver. The schools have been conducted prosperously ever s'nce under the direction of the Hibernian Society of Baltimore.

Libraries and Galleries.

Libraries, Museums and Art Galleries play an important part in the educational resources of a city. Besides the Peabody and Maryland Institute libraries in Baltimore, should be enumerated the resources of the Athenæum at the corner of St. Paul and Saratoga streets. In this building the Mercantile Library Association has its rooms on the first floor. It is a circulating library of 25,000 volumes of general current literature. The membership is chiefly of persons in mercantile pursuits and employees. The library is open daily. The second floor is occupied by the rooms of the Maryland Historical Society, which has 3,500 volumes of material forming the basis of the history of Maryland and other States, including several hundred volumes of newspapers. The literary treasures of the Society are very valuable. The rooms contain, besides, original documents and writings of eminent men of colonial and revolutionary times, relics and curiosities. Among the relics is the famous Pulaski banner, wrought and presented to the gallant Pole by the Moravian nuns of Bethlehem, Pa.; also an original portrait of Lord Baltimore. On the third floor is a large collection of valuable paintings. Some of these works are large, and comprise copies of noted masterpieces. There are portraits also of Jerome Bonaparte and his wife, who was Miss Elizabeth Patterson of Baltimore. In the same building is a collection of casts and statuary, representing many antiques. The collection, though not large, is well worth a visit. There is no charge for admission to any part of the Athenæum.

Maryland Academy of Sciences. Among the most interesting objects of interest to Marylanders, especially is the Museum of the Maryland Academy of Sciences on Mulberry street, opposite Cathedral street. Here the energetic members of this scientific association have collected specimens of nearly all the many varieties of fishes found in Maryland waters, with geological and mineral specimens, animals, birds, insects, &c. The collection is probably more complete than that possessed in any other State. The Museum is free and open daily.

Art Galleries. Though there are no striking or conspicuous Public Art Galleries, taste for art is widely diffused in the community of Baltimore, where, it has been seen, the means for cultivation begins with the lowest grades of public schools. A number of citizens have very large and valuable private collections. One of these is Mr. Wm. T. Walters, No. 65 Mt. Vernon Place, who possesses probably a collection not surpassed for quality in any other American city. His gallery is superbly fitted; comprises about 170 first class works, including specimens of Delaroche, Breton, Hubner, Calame, Desgoffe, Van Marcke, Frere, Boughton, Gleyre, Gerome, Schreyer, Plassan, Jimenez, Zamacois and others.

It is designed to make the Art Gallery of the Peabody Institute equal to the Corcoran Gallery in Washington. In addition to the endowment resources of the Peabody, public spirited citizens have already contributed liberally towards this end, among them Mr. John W. Garrett, who has given $15,000 to procure casts of the leading works of antiquity, to be ready for use by the time the additional buildings, now in process of erection, are completed.

Churches.

Where there are so many churches, it is not deemed essential to do more in the limited space of this book than to name the most conspicuous of each of the leading denominations.

Denomination.	Location.	Pastors.
Baptist	Eutaw Place	Richard Fuller.
Catholic	Cathedral, Cathedral st	Archbishop Bayley.
Evang. Lutheran	Fremont and Lanvale sts.	J. H. Barclay.
Methodist Epis.	Mount Vernon Place	J. O. Peck.
Methodist South	Fayette, near Republican	S. K. Cox.
Methodist Ind.	Lexington and Calhoun	R S. Moran.
Methodist Prot.	Poppleton street	S B. Southerland.
Presbyterian	Madison and Park sts.	J. C. Backus.
" Associate Ref.	Fayette street	John Leyburn.
Prot. Episcopal	Charles and Saratoga sts	J. S. B. Hodges.
Reformed Epis.	Bolton, near Lanvale st	Wm M. Postlethwait.
Swedenborgian	Calvert, north of Chase st.	W. G. Day.
Unitarian	Franklin and Charles sts	C. R. Weld.
Universalist	Balt st., near Central av	G. W Powell.
Hebrew Synag'e	Lexington street	Dr. Jacob D. Mayer.

The corner stone of the Cathedral was laid in 1806 by Bishop John Carroll. It was dedicated in 1821, and all debts having been paid, was consecrated May 25th, 1876. The first provincial council of American Bishops in 1829, and all subsequent councils up to the first Plenary Council in 1866, were held in the Cathedral. The founder, Bishop Carroll, was the first American Bishop, and the See of Baltimore has ever since been the chief See of the Catholic Church in the United States. The building has all the characteristics of a grand and imposing Cathedral.

The First Presbyterian Church, corner of Park and Madison streets, is of brown stone, with towers rising from the pavement, in graceful lines. The spire is 268 feet high, and the side towers 78 and 128 feet high.

Mount Vernon Place M. E. Church has been built five or six years. Its spire is nearly as lofty as the Washington Monument, near which it rises. The material is different colored stone and the architecture strikingly beautiful.

Other churches conspicuous for architecture are Christ Church, Prot. Episcopal, corner of St. Paul and Chase streets; Eutaw Place Baptist Church; St. Peter's P. E. Church, corner of Druid Hill avenue and Lanvale street; Franklin Square Presbyterian Church; Brown Memorial Presbyterian Church, corner of Park avenue and Dolphin street, and the First English Lutheran Church, Fremont and Lanvale streets.

Theatres.

Six theatres afford lyric and dramatic entertainment. These places of amusement are all reached by the different lines of street cars.

The most imposing "temple of the drama" in the city is the Academy of Music, a magnificent new structure on North Howard street, near Franklin street. The Academy was opened January 5th, 1875; its cost was something over $400,000. The main auditorium has a seating capacity of 2,000. The vestibule is very large, with cafes on each side, over which is a foyer or music hall 80x100 feet. The whole building is 102x250 feet, handsomely furnished and decorated, and lighted by electricity. The acoustic qualities of the theatre are perfect; the stage is large and scenery good. The seats are iron-folding arm chairs.

5*

Ford's Grand Opera House, Fayette street near Eutaw street and the Holliday street Theatre opposite the City Hall are also new buildings provided with all modern conveniences. Both theatres are under the management of Mr. John T. Ford. The Opera House has a seating capacity of 2,000 and the Holliday 1,500.

Front street Theatre, Front street, near Gay street, is the only old theatre left standing as a connecting link between the past and the present of the stage.

Concordia Opera House, is a German theatre, containing in the same building the club rooms of the Concordia Society, a rich association of the wealthier German citizens. The building was erected in 1865-6, and is a very handsome structure on South Eutaw street, near Baltimore street.

The Central Theatre is a new variety theatre near the bridge on East Baltimore street.

Business and other Places.

The Post Office and Custom House are in the Government Building, bounded by Second, Gay and Lombard streets.

Exchange Reading Rooms—entrances from Exchange Place and Second street, between South and Gay streets.

Corn and Flour Exchange, cor. South and Wood sts.

Board of Trade, office New Exchange Building.

Signal Service Weather Observation Office, corner of Second and Water streets.

Masonic Temple, North Charles street, near Saratoga.

Odd-Fellows Hall, North Gay street, near Fayette.

Germania Club, No. 181 West Fayette street.

Maryland Club, N. E. cor. Franklin and Cathedral sts.

Allston Association, N.E. cor. Franklin and Charles sts

Wednesday Club, No. 44 North Charles street.

University of Maryland School of Medicine, Greene and Lombard streets.

Washington University School of Medicine, Calvert and Saratoga streets.

Baltimore College of Dental Surgery, Eutaw and Lexington streets.

Maryland Dental College, No. 42 N. Calvert street.

Maryland Penitentiary and Jail, Madison street east of Buren street.

Bayview Asylum, (Almshouse,) Eastern avenue extended, between the Philadelphia and Mount Carmel Cemetery roads.

Foreign Consuls.

Country.	Name.	Location.
Great Britain	D. Donohue	Exch. Read'g Rooms.
France	Count de Montcabrier	54 Franklin.
Spain	M. Y. Colon	44 Courtland.
Mexico	C. D. de Rafart	65 S. Gay.
Germany	W. Dresel	37 S. Gay.
Belgium	G. O. Gorter,	Camden & Sharp sts.
Russia	C. Nitze	7 South.
Italy	E. de Merolla	23 S. Gay.
Netherlands	Claas Vocke	100 S. Charles.
Sweden & Norway	J. A. Solberg	} 65 S. Gay.
Denmark	W. Erichson,	
Uruguay	P. de Murguiondo	77 Cathedral.
Argentine Rep	C. Morton Stewart	} 52 S. Gay.
Brazil	C. O. O'Donnell	
Portugal	Robert Lehr	29 S. Charles.
Chili and Peru	Washington Booth	6 S. Gay.
Nicaragua	Basil Wagner,	25 S. Gay.
Austria	J. D. Kremelberg	56 S. Gay.

City Railways.

Green Line, from city limits Pennsylvania avenue, to Philadelphia depot.

Red Line, from West end Baltimore street to Baltimore Cemetery.

Blue Line, from terminus Light st., to end of Charles st.

White Line, from Thames st. to Station, North ave.

Eutaw street and Camden depot, from Baltimore street to Camden depot.

Canton Line, from North avenue to Toone street.

Citizens' Line, from Druid Hill to Patterson Park.

Park avenue Line, from South and German streets to Mt. Royal Reservoir and Charles street avenue.

Single fares on city street cars uniformly 6 cents.

Suburban Railways.

Catonsville Railway, depot West end Baltimore street.

York Road Railway, from Baltimore and Holliday streets for Towsontown and Govanstown.

Baltimore, Peabody Heights and Waverly Railway, from North Charles street and Boundary avenue.

Baltimore, Calverton and Powhatan Railroad, connect with Red Line, West Baltimore street.

Baltimore and Hall's Springs Railway, from City Hall, North street to Darley Park and Hall's Springs.

Expresses.

Adams Express, office 164 West Baltimore street.

Pennsylvania R. R. Baggage Express, north-east corner Calvert and Baltimore streets.

McFarland, Stephenson & Co.'s Express, office 114 South Eutaw street.

McClintock's Baggage Express, Camden Station, Office, 149 West Baltimore street.

Virginia Express Company, Washington and Georgetown. Office, 128 West Lombard street.

Union Transfer Company Baggage Express. Office, 143 and 150 West Baltimore street.

Hotels.

Barnum's Hotel, Calvert and Fayette streets.
Carrollton Hotel, Baltimore, Light and German streets.
Eutaw House, Baltimore and Eutaw streets.
General Wayne Hotel, Baltimore and Paca streets.
Guy's Monument House,* Calvert and Fayette.
Gibbon's Hotel, Howard and Saratoga streets.
Howard House, Howard street, near Baltimore.
Maltby House, Pratt, between Charles and Light.
Mansion House, Fayette and St. Paul streets.
Miller's Hotel, Paca and German streets.
Mount Vernon Hotel,* 81 West Monument street.
Pepper's Hotel,* Baltimore street, near North.
Rennert House,* Fayette street, near Calvert.
St. James Hotel, Charles and Centre streets.
St. Clair Hotel, Calvert street, near Fayette.
Three Tuns Hotel, Pratt and Paca streets.
Marked thus * are European plan.

Banks.

National Bank of Baltimore, Balt. and St. Paul sts.
National Union Bank, Fayette st., east of Charles.
Franklin Bank, South street, opposite German.
Marine Bank, Gay and Second streets.
Far. & Merchants' Nat. Bank, Lombard and South sts.
Merchants' National Bank, Gay and Second streets.
National Mechanics Bank, Calvert and Fayette sts.
Com. and Farmers' Nat. Bank, Howard and German.
Western National Bank, Eutaw st. near Fayette.
Chesapeake Bank, corner North and Fayette streets.
Nat. Farmers and Planters' Bank, South and German.

Citizens' National Bank, Hanover and Pratt streets.
Howard Bank, Howard and Fayette streets.
Bank of Commerce, No. 26 South street.
People's Bank, Baltimore and Paca streets.
First Nat. Bank of Baltimore, No. 8 south Gay street.
Second Nat. Bank of Baltimore, 147 south Broadway.
Third Nat. Bank of Baltimore, No. 31 South street.
National Exchange Bank, No. 4 south Sharp street.
German Bank of Baltimore, Holliday and Baltimore.
Old Town Bank, Gay and Exeter streets.
German American Bank, No. 173 South Broadway.
United German Bank, Baltimore st. and Post Office av.
Drovers and Mechanics' Bank, Balt. and Carey sts.
German Central Bank, Raine's Building.
Traders' National Bank, German and Light streets.

There are eight Savings Banks, having an aggregate of sixty or seventy thousand depositors, and twenty or twenty-five millions of dollars on deposit.

Telegraphs.

Western Union—Principal office, south-west corner Baltimore and Calvert streets.

Branches—Carrollton Hotel; Mount Vernon Hotel; corner Pennsylvania avenue and Townsend street; Howard House; Eutaw House; Wilhelm's Hotel, drove yards; Calverton Hotel, drove yards; Stock Board, No. 12 South street; Corn Exchange, South street; No. 78 Light-street wharf; Locust Point; Boston street, Canton; No. 39 South street; Jackson's wharf, foot Bond street; President street Depot; Union Depot; Camden Station; Fulton Depot; Mount Clare Station; Calvert Station.

Franklin—Offices, 131 West Baltimore street; No. 32 South street; Eutaw House; corner St. Paul and

Baltimore streets; corner Hanover and German; corner Gay and Lombard streets; No. 58 Exchange place; Alice Ann and Boston streets, Canton.

Foreign Steamers.

Baltimore and Bremen Line, European Pier, Locust Point; office No. 9 South Charles street.

Baltimore and Liverpool Allan Line, same.

Beaver Line, Liverpool, European Pier, Locust Point; office Gay and Lombard streets.

Coastwise and Bay Steamers.

Boston and Providence Line, wharf and office foot of Long Dock, Centre Market.

Charleston, S. C., Steamers, office 45 South Gay st.

Savannah, Ga., Steamers, wharf and office foot of Long Dock.

Bay Line, Norfolk, Va., wharf and office Union Dock, foot of Mill street.

York River and Richmond, Va., Steamers, Pier 10, Light street.

Potomac River Steamers, Pier 10, Light street.

Ericsson Steamers via Canal to Philadelphia, Pratt and Light streets.

Patuxent River Steamers, Pier 8, Light street.

Wilmington, N. C., Steamship Line, corner Light and Hughes street, office 50 South street.

Newbern, N. C., Steamers, Pier 10, Light street.

Powhattan, Richmond and Petersburg Steamers, Pier 2, Light street.

Baltimore and Fredericksburg Steamers, Pier 9, Light street.

Eastern Shore Steamers to Lower Maryland and Eastern Shore of Virginia, foot of South street.

Maryland Steamboat Company, to Annapolis, West River, Easton, Oxford, Cambridge, Denton, and Wicomico and Piankatank rivers; Pier 3, Light street.

Chester River Steamers, Pier 7, Light street.

Sassafras River Steamers, Pier 6, Light street.

Daily Newspapers,

The American, S. W. corner Baltimore and South sts.

The Sun, S. E. corner Baltimore and South streets.

The Gazette, No. 106 W. Baltimore street.

Evening News, No. 133 Baltimore streets.

Baltimore Bee, No. 16½ North street.

German Correspondent, Balt. st. and Post Office av.

Wecker, (German,) No. 88½ Baltimore street.

Hackney Coach Regulations,

To or from Steamboat or Railroad Stations to any
Hotel or private House in any part of the city—
one passenger,. . . . . 75 cts.

For each additional passenger, ... 25 "

For each trunk, box or bag, sufficiently large to be
strapped on, ... 15 "

No charge for small parcels put in the carriage.

City. From any one point within the city limits to
another—one passenger, . . . 75 cts.

For each additional passenger, . . . 25 "

Time. For one hour, ... $1 50

For each additional hour, . . . 1 00

Same rates for all fractions of an hour, but no charge for
less than a quarter of an hour.

Evening and Night. For Hacks taken from the
stand to any part of the city, as follows :

From 1st of May to 3d September, inclusive, after
8 o'clock, P. M., for a single passenger, . . 75 cts.

If more than one, each . . . . , . 50 "

Like sum for returning.

From the 1st October to 30th April, inclusive, after 7
o'clock, P. M., the same. No charge for baggage.

General Rules. 1. An additional allowance fo
carriage only when sent from stand, 25 cents.

2. Children over ten years, half price; under ten, no charge.

3. The Police force are strictly enjoined to enforce these
Rules.

Distances from Baltimore.

Places.	Miles.	Places.	Miles.
Annapolis, Md	38	Leavenworth, Kan	1,277
Altoona, Pa	217	Lynchburg, Va	218
Alexandria, Va	47	Martinsburg, W. Va	100
Augusta, Ga	709	Macon, Ga	885
Atlanta, Ga	762	Mobile, Ala	1,065
Boston, Mass	420	Montgomery, Ala	899
Buffalo, N. Y	431	Memphis, Tenn	971
Covington, Ky	647	Norfolk, Va	190
Cambridge, Md	90	New York City	188
Cumberland, Md	178	New Haven, Conn	262
Cincinnati, O	589	New Orleans, La	1,223
Charlottesville, Va	157	Parkersburg, W. Va	383
Charleston, S. C	600	Pittsburg, Pa	328
Chicago, Ill	830	Philadelphia, Pa	98
Danville, Va	311	Portland, Me	530
Erie, Pa	426	Providence, R. I	374
Elmira, N. Y	256	Petersburg, Va	193
Frederick, Md	61	Richmond, Va	170
Frostburg, Md	195	Savannah, Ga	704
Fredericksburg, Va	109	San Francisco, Cal	3,263
Fort Wayne, Ind	654	Staunton, Va	193
Grafton, W. Va	279	St. Louis, Mo	931
Galveston, Texas	1,711	Vicksburg, Miss	1,302
Hagerstown, Md	103	Washington, D. C	40
Havre de-grace, Md	36	Westminster, Md	36
Harrisburg, Pa	85	Wheeling, W. Va	379
Harrisonburg, Va	152	Wilmington, Del	70
Hartford, Conn	829	Winchester, Va	113
Lancaster, Pa	85	Wilmington, N. C	418
Louisville, Ky	696		

Baltimore to Philadelphia.

98	Baltimore.	0	40	Newark.	58
79	Magnolia.	19	28	Wilmington.	70
62	Havre de Grace.	36	14	Chester.	84
52	North East.	46	12	Ridley Park.	86
46	Elkton.	52	0	Philadelphia.	98

Baltimore Depots: President street and Charles street.

All steel rail double tracks, entering the Centennial Grounds at West Philadelphia and Philadelphia at Broad and Prime streets.

Time on Limited Express, 2h. 39m., and on Express trains, 3h. 40m. to 4h.

Stemmer's Run. Leaving the depot and passing in fine view of the harbor, the first station on the road is Stemmer's Run, a favorite resort for fishing parties.

Middle River, at the head of "the necks," the headquarters of the Maryland Yacht Club, and a favorite locality on account of the fine duck shooting between the months of October and January, and early in the Spring. Middle River is one of the feeding grounds of the famous canvas-back duck.

Edgewood, 21 miles from Baltimore, the nearest point to Belair, the seat of Harford county.

Bush River, 25 miles; a much frequented section for shooting and fishing.

Havre de Grace, 36 miles, on the west side of the Susquehanna river, the terminus of the Chesapeake and Tide Water Canal, and a large coal and lumber depot connected with Port Deposit, five miles above on the river. From this point the fine railroad bridge of thirteen spans, seven of them of iron superstructure, crosses the Susquehanna to Perryville, a distance of 250 feet. The bridge is fifty feet above the water, and although double tracks are laid, two trains are not permitted to pass over at the same time. No foot passengers are allowed to cross the bridge, but the trains are free, by law, to all for crossing. Grand views of the river above, and a wide prospect of the mouth of the river as it empties into Chesapeake Bay are presented. The river was formerly crossed by transferring trains on a ferry boat, which was the first of the kind ever constructed. The present bridge is built on great granite piers constructed by coffer dams and was completed in 1866. Between the Susquehanna and Baltimore, Back river, Gunpowder river and Bush river are crossed on long trestle bridges.

North East, at the head of North East river, 4C miles from Baltimore, the locality of the extensive McCullough Iron Works.

Elkton. The seat of Cecil County, Maryland, situated at the head of the Elk river and four miles west of the boundary line between Maryland and Delaware.

Newark. The first station on the Road in Delaware.

Wilmington. Originally a Swedish settlement, now the most important city in the State of Delaware. It is on Christiana Creek just above its junction with the Brandywine river, and the upper part of the city is 110 feet above the tide commanding an extensive view of the Delaware river. It is noted for its manufactures, which include seven flour mills that grind a million and a half bushels of wheat annually, a large powder mill, cotton factories, a paper mill, several woolen factories, seven iron foundries, and iron steamship works that turn out fifty iron steamers in a year. Iron ship building is the greatest mechanical industry of the city. A historic relic of much interest is the Old Swedes' Church with its surrounding graveyard over 200 years old.

Chester. The oldest town in the State of Pennsylvania having been settled by the Swedes in 1643. It was originally called Upland. The precise spot is shown where William Penn landed here on his arrival from England. The building of iron steamships is carried on extensively. Six miles west of Chester, just beyond the line dividing Delaware and Pennsylvania, is Brandywine Creek the scene of the battle of Brandywine during the revolutionary war, where General Lafayette was wounded.

Ridley Park. A new and handsome station, 11 miles from Philadelphia with fine residences, a good hotel, and a magnificent view of Delaware Bay. This is the locality selected by the Knights Templar for their Centennial encampment and several thousand members of that order are expected to visit the place during the summer.

The Centennial Exhibition.

In Philadelphia this year the "great attraction" is of course the Centennial Exposition. The grounds are connected with the entire steam railway system of the country. The price of admission at the gates is 50 cents and the hours, from 9 A. M. to 6 P. M. except Sundays.

The site of the Exposition is Fairmount Park, west of the Schuylkill river and north of Girard and Elm avenues, on a plateau 90 feet above the river. The boundaries are South, Elm avenue from Forty-first to Forty-second streets; West, the Park drive to George's Hill, with the Concourse; North, Belmont drive from George's Hill to the foot of Belmont; and East, Lans-

downe drive from Belmont to Forty-first street. There
are thirteen entrances along the boundary drive. Fairmount Park itself has 3,000 acres.

The Exhibition Buildings proper are five in
in number :
Main Building, 21½ acres. Horticultural Hall, 1½ acres.
Art Gallery, 1¾ acres. Agriculctural Hall, 10 acres..
Machinery Hall, 14 acres. Total, 48¾ acres.

"Annex" buildings, made necessary for requirements
of exhibition space, cover 26¼ acres additional, making
about 75 acres in all covered by main exhibition buildings, which is the largest acreage of any previous Exposition. Vienna, in 1873, had 50 acres; Paris, 1867, 40½
acres ; London, 1862, 24 acres.

U. States Government Exhibition Building, 1½ acres.
Area of enclosed grounds, 236 acres.
Avenues and walks, 7 miles.
Total number of buildings 180.
Average distance between buildings, 550 feet.

The total cost of the Exhibition is set down as
$6,724,850. Of this $2,357,750 have been secured by
stock subscriptions, $330,000 by gifts, concessions and
interest, $1,000,000 appropriated by the State of Penn-
sylvania, $1,500,000 appropriated by Philadelphia and
$1,500,000 appropriated by Congress.

State Buildings, Arkansas, California, Connecti-
cut, Delaware, Illinois, Indiana, Iowa, Kansas, Maryland,
Massachusetts, Michigan, Minnesota, Missouri, Missis-
sippi, Nevada, New Hampshire, New Jersey, New York,
Ohio, Pennsylvania, Vermont, Virginia, West Virginia,
Wisconsin. .

Foreign Countries represented. Argentine
Republic, Austria, Africa, (orange free State,) Belgium,
6*

Brazil, Chili, China, Denmark, Egypt, France, German Empire, Greece, Hawaiian Islands, Italy, Japanese Empire, Mexico, Netherlands, Norway, Peru, Portugal, Russia, Spain, Sweden, Switzerland, Turkey, Tunis, Venezuela, United Kingdom and Colonies, embracing Bahamas, Bermuda, British Guiana, Cape of Good Hope, Canada, Jamaica, New South Wales, New Zealand, Greenland, South Australia and Victoria.

Foreign Buildings. Great Britain, 4; France, 4; Japan, 3; Spain, 3; Germany, Brazil, Sweden, Canada, Turkey, Morocco, Tunis, Chili, Austria, Natives of Jerusalem, 1 each.

St. George's House, headquarters of the British Commission, is provided with quarters for the various British Colonial Commissioners, viz.: Dominion of Canada, Victoria, New South Wales, Queensland, South Australia, Tasmania, New Zealand, Cape of Good Hope, Jamaica, Bermuda and the Bahamas.

The first Foundation Stone laid for the Centennial buildings was for Memorial Hall. This is a stone structure designed to remain hereafter. At the time this foundation was begun there was not a single building or even the material for any except Memorial Hall on the grounds. In the brief space of two years three green fields have been graded, divided by broad and beautiful walks, drained, laid out into graded plats, and the greater part of them covered with beautiful buildings, numbering about one hundred and eighty in all, and some of them structures which have brought into play an immense amount of money, labor and mechanical ingenuity.

Restaurants. The Great American, French, Restaurant of the South, German Restaurant, Vienna Bakery and Coffee House, and others.

Miscellaneous Buildings. The Women's Industrial Pavilion, Shoe and Leather Exhibition Building,
Brewer's Building, and separate structures in the interest
of other trades and a Photographic Gallery.

Memorial Monuments. To Religious Liberty,
by the Hebrews near the Art Gallery; Fountain of the
Catholic Total Abstinence Union of America, with
figures of Charles Carroll of Carrollton, Archbishop
John Carroll of Baltimore, Father Mathew and Com-
modore Barry; Columbus Monument, a colossal statue
to the discoverer of America.

The Maryland State Building, situated among
other State buildings, is a House of Call for the South.
The building contains parlors and exhibition rooms, and
a very fair representation of the mineral, agriculture and
water productions of the State, souvenirs of colonial and
revolutionary periods illustrating the history of the State,
&c. The industries of the State are exhibited in the
main buildings according to their character.

What to See in Six Days.

Take a room near the Centennial Exposition grounds
and commence on the first day by entering on Belmont
avenue, turn to the right and you are in the main building, with a day's work before you and a trip around the
world. Still keeping to the right, we enter Chili and the
Argentine Republic, which with Peru and the Orange
Free State form the first section, and contain much that
is of interest. Then the old nations of China and Japan,
with curious exhibits of bronzes, straw work, silk and
mattings. Next Denmark, then Turkey and Egypt, followed by the beautiful pavilion of Spain and the exhibits

of Russia, Austria, Hungary and the German Empire united, and one-fourth of the day's work has been accomplished. We are now in the centre of the building, and if tired can rest and listen to the music of Gilmore's band, or push on to the exhibits of our own country, which occupy fully one-fourth of the main building. On arriving at the extreme end, go up in the gallery and view the wonderful vista which extends for nearly half a mile before the eye.

Returning, we leave the United States and passing through Mexico, the Netherlands, Brazil, Belgium and Switzerland, reach France and England, where hours can be spent with pleasure and profit. Then passing through Canada, Australia, Sweden, Norway and Italy, we have reached our starting point, and the bell chimes give notice that it is 6 o'clock, and time to close. Tired, we go to our hotel for a rest, and then if so inclined spend the evening at Operti's Garden, or go down in the city and visit Independence Hall, and thus has passed the first day. The second day should be devoted to the Machinery Hall, the Shoe and Leather Building, the Glass Factory, and the buildings in the vicinity. The third day visit the Art Gallery and its annexes, the Photographic Gallery and the Carriage Building, with a look at Judges' Hall. The fourth day can be pleasantly spent by a visit to the Government Building, the Women's Pavilion, the Model of Paris and the State Buildings. The fifth day can be given to the Horticultural and Agricultural Buildings. Devote the sixth day to an examination of the smaller buildings. Then take a boat up the Schuykill, visit the Zoological Gardens, Fairmount Park, the Wissahickon, and spend the evening at the Academy of Fine Arts, and the week has passed with both pleasure and profit.

Baltimore to Annapolis.

Routes by rail, Balt. & Ohio and Potomac roads.

By water, steamers from Light street piers.

Excursions from Baltimore or Washington to Annapolis and return, may be made in one day with ample time for observation.

Excursions from Baltimore to Annapolis by water are almost daily during summer, affording excellent opportunity for seeing the Chesapeake bay.

Annapolis, the capital of Maryland, was settled in 1650 and incorporated 1708. Many stately old colonial mansions built before the revolution still remain.

The State House fronts east and commands a magnificent sweep of the fine harbor and bay. Its surrounding grounds slope on the sides and front, and are well kept. The State House was built in 1773, and is a large old brick building of fine architectural proportions, the dome rising 200 feet from the ground, forming a conspicuous landmark above the surrounding houses on approaching the city from the bay.

The legislative halls, separated by a lofty and spacious rotunda, occupy the first floor of the building. The Executive Chambers and Court of Appeals rooms are in the second story, and the State Library, is on the west side of the building and contains 40,000 volumes. The Hall of the House of Delegates is very plain. The Senate Chamber, a smaller apartment, is tastefully furnished. In this chamber, in 1783, General Washington resigned his commission. A painting on the walls illustrates the event. There are also portraits of Charles Carroll of Carrollton, Samuel Chase, William Paca and Thomas Stone, the four Maryland signers of the Declaration of Independence, and John Eager Howard. An historical painting by Charles Wilson Peale, in which Washington and his aides-de-camp, La Fayette and Tilghman are represented, hangs in the Hall of Delegates. There are portraits of the Governors in the Executive Chamber.

One of the most interesting works of art in Annapolis is a colossal bronze statue on granite pedestal, of Roger B. Taney, late Chief Justice of the United States, by Rinehart, the Maryland sculptor. The statue was erected by the State of Maryland. It is directly in front of the main entrance to the Capitol. The Chief Justice is represented in a sitting posture, and the sculptor has inspired the bronze features with a cast of profound meditation.

The Executive Mansion, a short distance west of the State House, is a new brick house, large and commodious, surrounded by ample grounds. Its present occupant is John Lee Carroll, grandson of Charles Carroll of Carrollton.

The United States Naval Academy, School for cadet-midshipmen and engineers is on the Severn river on the northern boundary of Annapolis. The grounds comprise 50 acres, beautifully laid out and the buildings are numerous and handsome. On the water front and at the piers, training ships, monitors, and other war vessels lie moored or at anchor. The " Old Chapel," or museum of implements of warfare is open to visitors, and contains besides trophies of naval victories, a fine collection of weapons, specimens of naval machinery, models of famous war vessels. Among the trophies is a cannon that belonged to Cortez brought from Mexico, mementos of Perry's victory on Lake Erie and of the recent brush with the Coreans.

Other Public Buildings in Annapolis are St. John's College, founded in 1784; St. Anne's Protestant Episcopal Church; St. Mary's Catholic Church; the Redemptorist College, which includes in its buildings the old mansion of Charles Carroll of Carrollton; and the old Assembly Rooms.

Baltimore to the Blue Ridge Mountains.

WESTERN MARYLAND RAILROAD DISTANCES.

92	Baltimore,	0	44	Frederick Junction,	48
81	Greenwood,	11	24	Blue Ridge,	68
73	Reisterstown,	19	6	Hagerstown,	86
59	Westminster.	33	0	Williamsport,	92

Time: Through Passenger, 4h., 40m. Depot, corner Hillen and Exeter streets.

On account of elevation and purity of atmosphere, numerous summer resorts have been established on the line of the Western Maryland Railroad. Mount Hope Asylum is seven miles from the city on this line. Greenwood is an extensive excursion ground; Westminster, a thriving town surrounded by numerous dairy farms; Avondale, 36 miles from Baltimore, the seat of one of the largest nail factories in the country.

Emmittsburg, connected with the Western Maryland Railroad at Rocky Ridge, by a branch Railroad seven miles long, is a great summer resort from Baltimore. The society is refined and cultivated; population 1,500. Mount St. Mary's College and St. Joseph's Academy, both extensive educational institutions are situated near Emmittsburg in view of charming mountain scenery.

Many points along the line of the Western Maryland Road afford magnificent mountain views. Among the interesting points are Sabillasville, where the grade is 90 feet to the mile and the track half encircles the town, as the rails wind around the mountain side.

Blue Ridge, 68 miles from Baltimore, is 1,400 feet above tide, with accommodations for excursionists. Waynesboro', 71 miles from Baltimore, affords a magnificent view of the Cumberland Valley, Pennsylvania. Hagerstown is the county seat of Washington county and a delightful place of residence. At Williamsport, the railroad strikes the Potomac river and the Chesapeake and Ohio Canal. The town is one of the oldest in the State, and was the home of General Otho Williams, of revolutionary fame.

Baltimore to Washington City.

Washington City, by reason of the quickness of railroad communication by two lines and upwards of twenty trains each way daily, is practically a suburb of Baltimore. An excursion to the national capital by the Baltimore and Potomac Railroad brings the visitor to the Sixth Street Depot in Washington near the centre of the city. By the Baltimore and Ohio Line, the depot is only a short distance from the Capitol which is one of the first objects of interest. Street railway lines connect with both depots, and with all the public buildings and other important places, as indicated generally by signs on the cars.

All the Public buildings are open to visitors, and every public officer from President and Cabinet down, is accessible on business in business hours. The President receives business calls from 12 M. to 3 P. M., except on Tuesdays and Fridays which are cabinet days. Calls "to pay respects," should be indicated on the card, and the visit limited to two or three minutes. Evening receptions are held at stated periods during the winter to which all persons are privileged and there are no restrictions as to dress. On Saturday afternoons in summer, the Marine Band gives concerts at the President's grounds.

Afternoon receptions at the Executive Mansion are held by the ladies from 2 to 5 P. M., on stated occasions, and strangers and others are at liberty to go. No invitations are sent out.

The Capitol, which crowns a commanding eminence known as Capitol Hill, presents a magnificent facade to the east. The main entrance is on this side, though that most used is on the west side, on account of accessibility from the principal built up section of the city. The Navy Yard is southeastwardly from the Capitol on the eastern branch of the Potomac, and is reached by street cars from the Capitol grounds.

The Rotunda of the Capitol, which is the first place entered from the main entrances, east and west, presents numerous large historical paintings.

In going through the eastern main entrance the visitor passes several grand allegorical groups of statuary, one representing Columbus holding the globe in his hand, and the other a scene in border Indian warfare. A colossal statue of Washington stands in the park facing the east front. It is inscribed " First in war, first in peace, first in the hearts of his countrymen."

Free access is given to the chief halls of the Capitol, xcept the floors of Congress and within the bar of the

7

Supreme Court. Galleries are provided for the public in the Hall of Representatives and the Senate Chamber and there are doorkeepers to direct visitors through the lobbies. The Supreme Court is in the old Senate Chamber. The old Hall of the House is the depository of statuary, &c., contributed by the States. Indeed the Capitol, inside and outside presents a great array of works of art, too numerous to mention here. The Congressional Library, open from 9 A. M. to 4 P. M. daily, except Sundays, has 340,000 volumes. The only restrictions on the use of the books are, that they must not be carried away or defaced.

From the dome of the capitol a panorama of the Potomac, the city and surroundings is presented.

The President's Mansion, or the White House, is on Pennsylvania avenue, between 15th and 17th streets, northwest, fronting Lafayette Square, a little over a mile west of the capitol. The East Room of the White House is open daily, except Sundays, from 10 A. M. to 3 P. M. This room is the grand recepiton chamber. The Green, Blue and Red Rooms connect with each other and are used on public occasions. The accommodations for the President's family are in the western end of the house, and that part of the building is therefore closed to the public. The President's offices and secretaries are on the second floor, west end. The bronze equestrian statue of General Jackson by Clark Mills is one of the leading objects of interest of the square opposite the Executive Mansion. The surrounding grounds are magnificently laid out.

Public Places in Washington. Treasury Department, Pennsylvania ave. and 15th street.

State, War and Navy Departments, west of President's House, on 17th street near Pennsylvania avenue.

Washington Monument, S. W. of President's House.

Naval Observatory, E street, corner 24th street, northwest, on the banks of the Potomac towards Georgetown. The time of the City and Government is regulated here, and the latitude and longitude of the Western Hemisphere calculated.

The Patent Office, on account of its models and relics, is the chief attraction of the Department of Interior, located on the square bounded by 7th, 9th, F and G streets, northwest.

Post Office Department.—Square bounded by E and F streets and 7th and 8th streets. Entrance E street.

Smithsonian Institution, within the area of the New Park west of the Capitol and south of Pennsylvania avenue. Reached by 7th street cars. The grounds cover twenty acres. The national museum is the most interesting feature of the Institution and contains specimens from many exploring expeditions.

Department of Agriculture, in the Mall, south of Pennsylvania avenue, between 12th and 14th streets.

Corcoran Art Gallery, northeast corner Pennsylvania avenue and 17th street, opposite the War Department. Entrance from Pennsylvania avenue. Picture galleries, 2d story. Main Hall of Statuary and Bronzes, 1st floor.

The Gallery is open every day, (Sundays and certain holidays excepted,) from 10 A. M. to 4 P. M., from October 1st to May 1st, and from 10 A. M. to 5 P. M. from May 1st to October 1st.

Tuesdays, Thursdays and Saturdays, admission free.
Mondays, Wednesdays and Fridays, admission 25 cts.

Mondays, Wednesdays and Fridays only, persons will be admitted, under certain regulations, to the privilege of drawing from casts and copying the pictures.

Children under six years of age will not be admitted to the Gallery, and none under fourteen years will be admitted, unless accompanied by grown persons.

The City Hall is surrounded by Judiciary Square, fronting Louisiana avenue at the head of 4½ street between 4th and 5th streets. The Arsenal, where the Lincoln conspirators were tried, lies south, at the other extremity of 4½ street.

Army Medical Museum, in the building which was a Theatre, where President Lincoln was killed. The museum is on the 3d floor and contains an immense number of specimens of especial interest.

Ordnance Museum, F and 17th streets, contains captured flags, and many military curiosities.

Congressional Conservatory, west side of the capitol grounds and south of Pennsylvania avenue, filled with rare plants and foliage, flowers, &c. Free.

The Congressional Burial Ground, Eastern Branch of the Potomac, 1½ miles from the capitol.

The Navy Yard, Eastern Branch of the Potomac, is interesting for its collection of guns, trophies, ship houses, workshops, war vessels, monitors, &c.

Government Hospital for the Insane, two miles south of the capitol, on the south side of the Eastern Branch, reached by Pennsylvania avenue, and the Anacostia Bridge.

The Arsenal is the extreme southern limit of the city at the mouth of the Eastern Branch. Curiosities from battle-fields, &c., are exhibited. The entrance to the Arsenal grounds faces 4½ street.

Georgetown is three miles west of the capitol, and separated from Washington by Rock Creek. It is the seat of Georgetown University and the Academy of the Visitation, two of the oldest Educational Institutions in the country, and is a flour, fish and coal market of importance. The Georgetown Heights afford a magnificent view of the river and surrounding country. A line of street cars runs directly from the capitol to Georgetown.

Arlington, the estate of General R. E. Lee, is directly opposite Georgetown, on the south bank of the Potomac. It is now a National Cemetery, where the remains of 15,590 soldiers are buried.

The Soldiers' Home, a beautiful drive and pleasant place to visit, is on Rock Creek.

Alexandria, on the through route to Richmond, Va., is seven miles distant from Washington. There is a Steam Ferry from the foot of 7th street, and cars from 6th street depot cross the Long Bridge. By the Baltimore and Ohio route, cars run down the east side of the Potomac and cross on barges at the ferry to Alexandria.

Mount Vernon. Steamboats ply daily between Washington, Alexandria and Mount Vernon, the home and grave of Washington. It is a pleasant trip from Baltimore to Mount Vernon and return the same day.

Baltimore to Niagara Falls.

The Northern Central Railway is the great route from Baltimore, through Pennsylvania and New York to Niagara Falls and Lake Erie. The scenery along the entire line is magnificent.

Leaving Calvert Street Station or Charles Street Depot, the traveler passes the great Machine Shops of the Company near the city's boundary, and through numerous villages to Lake Roland, over the Gunpowder river, through the marble region of Baltimore county to Hanover Junction connecting with Gettysburg, the celebrated battle-field and a noted watering place, 46 miles from Baltimore. The other notable points on the route are :

York, Pennsylvania, a thriving inland town, the locality of the Company's Car Shops, 57 miles from Baltimore.

Harrisburg, 84 miles from Baltimore, the capital of Pennsylvania. The Susquehanna River near Harrisburg affords some of the finest scenery along the line.

Williamsport, Pennsylvania, the centre of the great lumber trade of the region, 178 miles, and Elmira, 256 miles from Baltimore.

Watkins, New York, 278 miles from Baltimore, on Lake Geneva, a beautiful town, remarkable for its picturesque situation and localities, its famous Glens, hill and lake scenery. Watkins is a favorite stopping place on the route to Niagara.

Niagara Falls, 431 miles from Baltimore.

Baltimore to Richmond.

The Baltimore and Potomac Railroad traverses the five lower counties of the Western Shore of Maryland, to Pope's Creek on the Potomac River, 73 miles. The Washington Branch from Baltimore to Washington was opened in 1872, and was followed by connections with Southern lines to Richmond, Va. The traveler can leave Baltimore in the morning, go to Richmond and remain one hour and return by 10.30 P. M. the same day.

Baltimore to the West.

Baltimore and Ohio Railroad from the Atlantic Coast to Chicago is 795 miles; St. Louis, 918; Louisville, 688; Cincinnati, 578; Pittsburg, 327. The total length of track of the road and branches is 2,460 miles, extending in seven states: Maryland, West Virginia, Pennsylvania, Ohio, Indiana, Illinois and Missouri. Among the notable points for scenery and summering are the Relay House, Ellicott City, Harper's Ferry, Cumberland, Frostbnrg, Deer Park, Oakland, Cheat River, Berkeley Springs, &c.

The Pennsylvania Railroad route to the West is characterized by superb equipment, wayside accommodations and beautiful scenery. From Baltimore, by the Northern Central Railway, to Harrisburg, where the route strikes the valley of the Juniata to Altoona, the site of numerous car shops and railroad works; thence up the grade of the Alleghany Mountains, via Cresson, with its magnificent scenery, to Pittsburg. From this point passengers have the choice of two routes to the great West, viz: by the Pan Handle to Cincinnati; or by the Fort Wayne and Chicago road.

www.ingramcontent.com/pod-product-compliance
Lightning Source LLC
Chambersburg PA
CBHW021534270326
41930CB00008B/1240